THE BEAR WITHIN

Poems by
Wing Williams

be ye not afraid
of the wild truth within
sharpen it with life

Copyright © 2016 by David Kelly Williams who is Wing.

All rights reserved. Other than brief passages or quotes in a newspaper, magazine, book in reference, radio, television review, internet review, or documentary, no part of The Bear Within may be reproduced in any form, through any mode, electronic or mechanical which includes recording or photocopying or any other type of information storage and retrieval system without written permission from the author David Kelly Williams.

Manufactured in the United States of America

Williams, David Kelly
Williams, Wing

ISBN-13 978-0-9981127-0-1

Contents

Altar in the Sky   3
Visions of Ol Reelfoot   6
Breaking New Grounds   8
Many Mentors   9
When Winter Wears Black   10
Escape to Reality   11
North Breakfast North   12
Basics   13
Pickles and Beer   15
The Beginning of a Brotherhood   17
Granny Jones   21
Stuff   22
No Hiatus   25
Go to the Desert Boy   27
To Breathe Again   28
With the Strings   29
To the Land of the Human
   and Back Again   30
A Quiet Sit   33
A Blurry Perhaps   34
Day Near Done   35
Mountain Morning   38
Cry with the Weight Smile
   with the Wait   40
The Ivory   42
Gentleness   43

Coffee and a Cigarette   45
A Sleep Beneath the Willows   46
Day Two   47
Kiss   50
Remember You   52
Jacob   53
Midnight Jaunts   60
Hideaway   61
Kid from the Shire   62
The Commons   63
Then   64
September   65
Son of a Father   66
Portsmouth Fire   67
Dab City   68
Caribou Hill   70
Bang Bang   71
Cattail Wallows   73
Red Ribbon Haze   74
An Art Thought a Life Goal   75
Puddle Straw   76
No Buttons   77
The Routine of Two Feet   79
Father   83
No Light Upon my Porch   84
Night with the Devil   85
Daughter of Eternal Clocks   87
Symphony of Youth   89

Cling to Life   90
Poem Box   93
Little Woodland Savage   95
Poison Ivy on a Good Day   98
The Singing Tree   99
Stand and Listen   101

For Marion Kelly Williams Jr.
MY FATHER

Altar in the Sky

the mountain has awoken
dragon heart beating
ominous crescendo
volcano cadence
deep from her innards
beyond my left ear

I clutch the earth laying as I was born
within her breast is the soul of this storm

alchemist lungs create
vulgar steam illuminated by
fire webs in the sky
beyond my tent walls flash
great dazzles of light
unveiling ice axe and crampons
down beyond my toes
into the occasional ebony
still alive
I throw them far

-metal clink upon sharp lava rock

screams of the stars
frozen upon their fall
drum on wilting fortress
marbles of mountain dance
rejoicing rimy alien arrivals
storm settles into the onslaught
never threatened
by the peace of sun

to the west hours ago

> a drink for Mt Shasta
> cheers to The Queen!
> to the trail and our life
> dirty diamonds never seen
> by dead billboard eyes
> and robots of the street

a toast that bred warmth,
avowed earnest sleep

the Great White Angel pierces
my Cimmerian throne

-the bourbon holds no comfort now

sheer monopoly of sound
suffocates the droning hail
and whooping hawhees
of my two brothers wild
praying his own way

there is no choice but to wait

another light giant
swallows the night
another cannon of heavens
strikes a fiery saber too near

no silhouette of my friends the trees
far far below this once treeless peace

nothing but us in our colorful hobbles
three piles of molecules
orange upon coruscating obsidian
green within the caterwauling winds
yellow beneath the swallowed summit
one upon the chakras beating heart

this is but a test

Visions of Ol Reelfoot

He tread this was, perhaps
sat upon this same rock,
our ponderosa ridge
considering logs now dust.
The tree which supports my lean
bears forgotten musk.
Scent swims my sweaty nose
into blood stream,
Ah the tears
of brown majestic pilgrim beast.
Shoulders weary from weight
I rub them vigorously until
the comfort of sap upon an itch
relieved satisfies me
-as Ol Reelfoot would.
From the riverbank he would climb
to not share his meal,
to grunt after full body shake,
the mane of a last great
showering the cold former home
of his fish
upon my bearded face.
We have that in common
my lone wondering friend
-and that too.
Alone you would sleep
alone you would lumber
forever being chased
cross the scrub oak peppered land
into canyons down until
their fear returned

upon your haunting strength.

Oh Pilot Rock the haunts you bear
of the soul Ol Reelfoot
and his lost brother's despair.
He had a sister once he groaned
'til she was caught
and craftily sold
so why would he not grin to gnaw
on flesh of those
his righteous soul saw
as those who only trap and kill,
beat and bound the money they
taste.
Ah but as Ol Reelfoot was
as Pilot Rock still bears his blood
let me roam
for I am free,
if you hurt my sister
all your flesh I'll eat.

Rest easy my friend
your soul lives within me,
giant with a broken heart,
son of a mother
who left you to be the last great,
whispering legend with last loving
breath.
Would you lounge in the willows
and wonder,

why me?

Breaking New Grounds

ponderers
hungoverers

birds early
for coffee worms
a chance at new
day long stories

not,
I slept late and I feel greats

Grandfather   with
granddaughters
ivy looking leaguers
with pink patterned collars
smoke bummers
wet boot sloshers

the sun will unveil
her donned sunglasses tell
or look at me not
       is maybe her thought
-yes look at me not
       look at me not.

Many Mentors

it is below I do fly
tho here upon the phalanx of fir
I can kiss the sky

above the rugged under green
where precise tender toe touch
upon pine needles bring
my swift immortal run with the elk

Eyes Insatiable
Peripheral Hunger
Sage on Lion
Elder on Bear
Wolverine to Water

low I look up into this forest top
lounge
decided and able
I climb each bough to the crown
100 arms higher than where I glide
the eagle sits

chest broad to the wind
      chocolate back to the shine

            my roar of silence
            my glint in time
            my unabashed true

I sway with feathers and firs
listening to the blue.

When Winter Wears Black

with music we spent our time
a carnival of each's turns
    at guitars
        bongos
            keyboard
even an electronic beat mixer

together we played
together we thrashed

by the time the bread was ready
we were on our way to drunk,
honestly stoned
fingers calloused
friendly eye gazes long

but it was no matter

we poured another glass
lit another joint
piled the plates high
with bread and salad
soup bowls for all
many moments of silence to come

thankful for the friendship and food
to share

Escape to Reality

Mind and body race with feverish anticipation. I sit in a small crowded bus of 12 sweaty bodies each hugging carry-ons upon their tightly squeezed laps. After chugging past Mesquite in the Nevada desert a man leans awkwardly around to ask "What're you headed down here for son, the casinos are behind us."

"I am going to hike the Grand Canyon." I reply, looking forward, shamed to breathe directly into the woman's face to my left.

"The Grand Canyon eh, a lil escape from reality! I wish I could up and do something like that."

I smile, knowing that in fact I was in reality; I never sought to escape it, but merely find and commune within it. "You can." I tell him, and this time I turn my head and smile. Little does he know that my pockets jangle of only $13 in quarters to my name, and that is no bother.

North Breakfast North

Wakefield Diner
moose out front
wood brown never move
unless Nor Easter
is strong enough

breakfast kings
all line the booths
mountain mommas
remember names
as they pulse the blood
through my veins

there's always one
I could maybe marry
if I returned for more than
bacon
eggs
a cinnamon roll and coffee

simple laugh over
meaningful anecdote
an eager outdoor smoke
strap on the pack
hit the road lines
with thumb as the king

the wild is a lonely place
and that is where I'll be

Basics

Today I worked on basics.
Learned to identify a few more trees
I had previously been unsure of,
tho I miss the madrones and sugar maples
I observe the grandeur of this chandelier
with vigorous attentiveness.
Refreshed identification of bird calls
practice of this day primarily birds of prey;
between Red Tail and Cooper
Bald and Golden
Kestrel and Osprey.
It is important to fine tune ear such
be it mandolin or ukulele which tickles our brains.
Then onto other sweet refreshments
the wild edibles of this land,
must we beaver inner bark or roast choice roots
this too is crucial doctrine.
Though leontodon taraxacum be an always favorite
not just the sun sabered soothsayers shall suffice.
Elder, amaranth, bayberry, cattail, juniper, fireweed
as well,
we shall feast more fair than Oliver's city despair!
As the day passed,
my shade tarp creatively adorned different spaces
of air.
Dog n I,
run n fed,
beverages being drunk,
sun sets,
night awakens.
I salute Leo to the south,

Taurus to the west,
Polaris shining ever true
as the Great Bear watches over all,
birds now nested away
their songs not again 'til dawn,
an owl sits above.

Pickles and Beer

Crickets cannot drain
the boom of guns
shot in country night
far beyond the yellow field of weeds
near red barn that harbors dogs
trained to hunt
nor the alabaster scream
of a north bound train.
They, the crickets
sing in this night
though the sun
still alive in my skin.
Southern Georgia winds travel low
without wooden impedance
until they reach me
and my smoke
and my scalp
again alive with less winter hair
to shield from
the drenching shower
of that sun.
As night strengthens
the ground has become more alive
as a pen pissed steed
gallops in the dark
unsaddled
unbridled
yet not free.

Snakes slither through tall blades
of angry grass

beaten by winter winds
and sting sharp to dive
for the pop fly
hit by father
who too is a son
and was bellowing rich laughter
thinking rich memories
spitting the taste of pickles and beer.
I dive for the ball,
catch it and savor the sting
of this stubborn grass.
I stand and laugh
with him in return.

The Beginning of a Brotherhood

The sand was hot. Cooler beneath this sun shielding desert slab of road but still hot, pleasing upon bare calves in contrast to the quickly melting ice sack on right knee. Red ants march hot molecules of desert floor down my lower back into ripped grey sweat stained shorts to build little clay huts by my salty sea. With body born spice they meander, surely it tastes delightful though I care not for their personal tastes and aspirations, let them. We are all one in this sun scorched land, anything that breathes anything that thirsts, anything that hopes we are one.

Picking the plastic bag off swollen knee I hold it upon my weathered face. Water once frozen now drips into beard and rivers down my skin. The streams embrace with one last fading chill.

Before me, lies a dry creek bed flanked by beige withered grass baring no purples. Velvet reprieve of shade perhaps fifty feet long maybe thirty feet wide. Thankful for this once waterway, this flash flood zone, this crevasse which requires a short flat bridge for desert dwellers to drive upon seeking wet satisfaction on the coast two hundred miles west. This shade, this dry washed out piece of earth is where I will begin again. Here my mind gathers courage for tomorrow's walk of continue, continue new, for success, for life and green springs a marathon beyond the San Phillippe hills of hell.

Through the dry creek bed a rattlesnake slithers slow. Dark brown diamonds burrow into soft sand for a moments rest. The snake raises head slight seeing my orange glow four feet above. Friendly from afar with his respectful head nod and curious tongue flicker. He understands my slow heart beat nestled into cooler earth. After a rest he continues on into the unforgiving sun.

Head rests back upon the stone slab of occasional rumble, body calm with cannabis. Right knee still throbs; I smile for its throb is less, less than yesterday, less than 7 days before, less than the grapefruit it had become years ago in the humid jungle air of Carolina's western backcountry. I had begun the almighty change of how I walked and tomorrow will implement in true live free or die style my desert test – find my center again, walk with confidence again.

"You alright?" His voice pierces the silent save for the sand that nibbles my ear to the south. I turn. He stands, weight resting upon right foot, a hazy visage of sun sweating upon the melting earth. I smile.

"I'm Hot Wing."

"I mean are ya doing fine? You look like a bum kid."

"I am better than fine, this shade's doin a stellar job at hugging me, an earth hug ya know?" A shrug, he knows, but he just stands there in that damn sun as if my shade may infect him with the great disease of laziness and apathy. "Don't be scared of me shade me friend! What's your name?"

Looking north into the brown hills dotted with white boulders ahead he speaks, "I'm pressing on, a few more miles before dark, I may walk with the night, I may not." I nod as I roll a smoke.

"Well nice to meet you Pressing On." I chirp still waiting for his name, picking up pieces of fallen tobacco sticking to my sandy bare chest.

"My name is Samuel," dancing Mexican syllable on the end. A pause with the wind, "You walkin tonight Wing?"

"Not tonight," I light my smoke. "Ima sleep under this bridge and head out early in the morn before the sun eats the cool of night's end. Then I reckon I'll siesta under some sagebrush for a few hours midday before making the push for the springs. I'll be there by dark."

"See you tomorrow night then ya bum." He leaps with a laugh and hikes on. I return to my thoughts, watch the ant's zealous ferocity, choose an apple from my pack to eat between the drags of my desert smoke and drift into the nirvana of now.

Granny Jones

Well my goodness!
you just may be the tastiest apple
mine buds have ever versed
so tantalizing in your crunch
      that oozes juices
most seducing
down my consuming hearth

a fortress of power
amidst your castle of flavor
I can now
      heal   run   fly   love
with more savor

if only I could share you,
to have another true adore,
then together we could love far
clearer than afore

for the treasure in you apple

is unlike any other before

Stuff

Stuff.
The accumulation of stuff
how oddly necessary and not
my blue hat
acquired for 50 cents
10,000 mountain miles ago
bearing many dreams
oft upon my head,
50 cents could longer buy
my blue hat.
Necessary?
Yes,
morale   sun cover   artists canvas
summit scars   lovers play   grizzly
pursuit
elk mate or fight   dog love tares
n fireside sows,

this hat is where I'm at
this hat is where I goes.

However,
there are the things they carry
and there are the things that sit,
latter I do not think
have been valued correct.
First for true
Who made this for you?
Why was it purchased
when you already have two?
Perhaps it is a first

to use and appreciate.
Perhaps it is not?
Forget then such urge.
A wooden palate for rot
is my finest of tables.
Once considered
broken down
reassembled.
I see the beggar with bags
I see the artist with less
I see the large house of
man with too many threads,
no wonder he must have
and her too.
Stuff.
So much it floats in oceans
forgotten forever
so why look at it now…
To be nomadic or elite
to be content and obsolete
of a night without the purr
of a thousand machines at rest.
Yes purr on 'til you falter
I've more hours to spend
not under trees
to fix your dead purr again.
Media for breakfast
running machine at lunch,
I'll not join you for dinner
I've had enough.
Give me the rising sun,
resilient embers,
coffee in my one mug
from valley of Roan Highlands,

yes give me few stuff
forever may it hold
the stories of us,
Grandfather's flannel,
axe of desert dig n ice climb
bearing brothers forge,
the flint she gave,
guitar found with father's mother
midst saw mill pine land,
rifles in pawn shop,
men with goatees and short hair.
Who made this?
Why must I have it?
Thank you for the gift.
If it be right, we shall see each other
again.
This may be necessary
and then this may be not.
To each tis peculiar
as is this existence
we share.

No Hiatus

I see the face of a bear
magnificent cherry tree in dark
becomes his angry ruffled ears n hair

two shrubs make up those
black ready set bones high
eye sockets valleyed
twigs tangled thickets tight
as panda patches could

thru such nest the neighbor windows glimmer thru
      heat of eyes
        eyeball fury
a hunger tenacious 'til warm blood taste
sliver of amble wood to keep
the blazing fire aggress

white picket fence extends the two
low,
silhouette in full moon

perhaps it is how the shadows are set
but mine eyes see a beast snarling full press

      bare space above
      trunk of cherry for subtle nose

gnarled in the night light
my gaze not confused

his menace is a comfort
as my dark sits in no light

This is what I look at.
What do you see tonight?

Go to the Desert Boy

in the rain
the tourists still came
oblivious of the pain
a single girl untamed

for why should they think of it so

even I outside with a monocle eye
know now to think of it so

so outside I sit
always prepared to flit
away to where the tourists came
from

to the emptiness they leave behind

To Breathe Again

crash crash crash

through destruction I feel

push passion push
'til gone is too far
'til there is no return
from a misery of life

'This is not the way,' -he said.
'There is no moral in the
destruction.'

'No moral?' I replied.
'My morals
are on the towel over there.'

he looked to the ground

and I was gone

With the Strings

The poet sat beside the woman in bed,
her asleep
him shirtless
-smoke in hand.
Ava Maria sang the dying jay
and slavery of today
revolution always beat
to this poet's quick step
along rivers beneath waxing moon
as to be,
forever growth thru phase.
Tonight we have travelled
from sun shadow
through flirtatious exchange
I believe her heart when she sings
Oh Melena,
she is river ever stronger by
vigorous rising spring.

Look through the window
forget being angry for not being outside
it is hour for sleep they said
we've another world for you they say
I suppose so,
this delight, this warmth,
this sanctuary for butterfly soul
-slumber easy tonight ol hoss
despite the coyotes and elk now
further away
they shall sing for you, with you,
a carnival of animals.

To the Land of the Human and Back Again

For the first time in 5 days there was that rumble.
Dismissed by the breath of trees
by the crack of dead branches
beneath beasts who sniffed curious as I did so.
It was a road still miles away, north,
I must cross it I knew.
Descending into deciduous the roar of modern men
harshed by in stink of death trap.
They sought the bear in a way I did not.
A woman waved delighted by my hairs
her scent but a memory,
to show her the way I sought the bear…
Here by rusted sugar cans of government
along the asphalt dead
slicing through forests of living earth
my body was taken east down into the lands
nether of purity.
The humble tavern stood before me,
as McCarthy would say,
'there is no such joy in the tavern
as upon the road thereto.'
To prove him wrong I entered
for inside were woman and man
inside was camaraderie
perhaps they would understand.
She sat at the bar and lit a smoke,
her eyes invited me to join
her lips confirmed the invoke.
The 1st pint was on me
for these dirty dollars still worked,

2nd on her for she was intrigued by my plight,
3rd from the bartender who wanted me to stay
the 4th 5th and 6th by men who debated my ways.
"Let's hear him again!
Let's not lose another game,
another round for the mountain man!"
-a whiskey bottle now displayed.
Through laughter and ahh's over stories I told
each looked at me suspicious
never quite being sold
by my revelation of freedom on cold lonely nights,
of a mountain so holy why hide 'neath its shine.
"The trees are for harvest the bear for my wall."
My heart discouraged by what sullen ears heard,
I smoked another cigarette
not forgetting their curse.
Vision blurred my soul began to ache
so I grabbed up the bottle and yelled at the jerk.
"Where is the one who will join me up there?
Where is the one who dares to see
this poisonous destruction of truth!
You do not own it this land a gift for proper use.
Money has begot the devil in you."
My craze had returned,
only she smiled sweet,
they snatched up the cue sticks
with new idea for my fate.
I took one last long swig and smashed
the counter hard,
glass hit the ceiling
she now shrieked in regard.
Holding my weapon against the governments men,
in came the sheriff who had heard of my plan.
"Now son I think it's time you came with me."

I had but a moment,
his hand on his hip,
cue sticks set down,
shattered bottle still gripped,
there was no time to waste.
I threw the bottle cross the room
it hit the window with a shatter
the room became a den of jagged toothed sabers
hand to his gun I ran opposite of die
out the back exit by privy I knew
pack now in hand
up into the dark forest I again began.
Thorns tore at my skin
blood trickled into beard,
higher and higher 'til sweet pines beckon my near.
Never once did I stop 'til I was far above
upon that holy mountain
looking down down with love.
Tears mixed with sweat now greet red torn flesh,
into the ravines I howl
knowing only I
and the eagle
and the bear
and the trees
and the deer
and the coyote
can hear me now.
Beneath the sliver of moon
silver upon truth,
McCarthy was right,
sometimes it takes a tavern
to remember what is true.

A Quiet Sit

Robert Leon Roper Jr.

first rainbow gathering

Washington deli

LOTUS

blisters ooze yellow puss

feet popped into blood

flakes dead skin out of beard
white powder
but it aint

what here?
food some
plans not much
maybe Nevada
maybe Cali   heat

home from Oklahoma
on the streets
cold don't get along.

Cirrhosis

A Blurry Perhaps

"I once wrote a short story entitled
The Man Who Never Slept."
The 151 burned his throat as it settled deep,
she opened the door as he lit new words on fire,
snatching the story she would never read
into the white
she threw the hellish remains.
A blizzard carried the tune for the night.
"Did you now? Did you burn that story as well!?"
Retort amidst the buzz of adrenaline
and fiery intoxication.
She straddled his legs and sat upon his lap.
Her tulip lips of liquor sweet on his neck.
A nymph in throws of head back bottle up.
"No. I did not. I left the words in a bar
right where I got my drunk,
caused a little scene…
Was told to leave."
"Of course you did baby!"
She let the fire drip from her lips into his beard.
Hips sway to the fiddle that ran thru the snow
as did we.
Fire in her eyes,
fire in her hips,
fire in the bottle that kept them both lit.
"Dance with me" she purred as
her fingers drew blood from his chest.

Day Near Done

As expected in his corner he sat
      on wooden chair recently sanded
      by wooden desk never painted

two windows to look through.

Morning Glories embraced the sill asleep too
in the dark as I arrived home.

Mountains shrouded
by light swallowing beasts
no moon to kiss
the deepest intimacies of the gulch

His lump lit
by one stump candle
wax dripped long
forehead in palm
ol eyes closed to the honest ebony
beyond the frosted glass.

   "Cold in ere."   I stated to myself
                           to the dark
                           to my dormant friend

With satisfaction I lay down my pack
to gather small kindling,
an armful too of split firewood
drier than a July Mojave
      toils of mine hand,
      Earth's gift with intention

With light of the tinder each
participant crackled forth
upon this room in hibernation
upon the ol man asleep in the still.

Breath of life
the window panes groaned
another log upon greedy flames

the cat appeared stretching from
warm recesses of blankets n bones

the ol man grunts irregular
from his slothful drawls
warmth reaching him now
across the once sterile silence

in my chair, I sit
low and submissive
finally, to the ease
within the fortress of my gulch

"Welcome home Wing," I hear in low rumble

The Bear stands as he extinguishes his candle low
The Bear shuffles through the illumination
The Bear sits again -too at ease
opposite I upon the galaxy painted lounge

"Ol Man Sam," I smile, "how you doin my friend?"

"Good mon good."

He yawns as the bear would

gazing into the warmth
into the flame.

Mountain Morning

Early in the morning he awoke.
The moon still shined upon
the mountain he would climb soon,
his socks crisp with sweat from day before.
Northern messengers seeped
through wooden walls to remind his fingers
- this is why he awoke,
there would be no more delay,
it was a firewood day.
The kettle bred coffee and oatmeal,
he rolled three joints,
smoked one carried two.
With excitement in his dry lips
he sharpened the teeth of his blade,
oiled the saw,
inhaled
exhaled
remembered
shrugged
moved on.
Tied his boot laces high tucking in
each corner of longs
then into the dawn he began.
Truck stood cold waiting for the first sun rays
though the ignition still turned.
"Ol blue still gonna come through."
As he sat patiently peering
through the frost covered windshield,
fog of premonition evaded the day.
Up the dirt road they climbed
past the forgotten mine,

through the Aspen groves of gold,
into the pines of old
until no further could those wheels go.
Here he stepped out,
his feet nimble,
his mind and blade sharp.
It was a day he looked forward to each autumn,
a day he would repeat
until he could no longer swing an axe;
many dead trees to fall,
much wood to cut,
a long winter ahead.

Cry with the Weight
Smile with the Wait

snow is dripping through the trees
seems it cannot commit
it'd be rain if it pleased

I let the flakes hit my eyes
cold and crisp it sizzles
warmed by my eyeballs
the snow simply fizzles
into tears and down my cheeks
to my feet where gravity seeks

ahh a spring that stalks close behind
this stubborn winter
that shall not splinter
away from its grind

to bring about such a dark

a bone some chill and humbling
dark

to make us smile evermore

when day is finally greeted

by songs of the lark

Vampire Beauty

Queen of Clean

Lady of the Higher Mind

Enigma of My Dreams

The Ivory

To touch the ivory again,
dare delve into the trees of dark and silent fog
staccato to fields of endless long
'til tulips dawn is the axiom.

My head to rest inside rhythmic breaths
my soul to pour through fingers and kiss
the angered trap of muted mind.

The feeling untouched unless I do just this
and veritably undress the moor.

Have slept through moss and many fawns
so I must tame the dark
which I once knew how,

with a piano once again

with forgotten choice to lose known thoughts
to touch with life only I can nurture

as I would make love to a woman.

Gentleness

Penelope looked across the chipped stone table at Jack. He put out his cigarette in a crack and looked up at her with his eyes, deep into hers, begging her to not look away. "I know." Jack muttered quietly. She held his gaze. She loved his eyes. She wanted to kiss his sad eyes.

"I don't know how to escape it, it just happens, this time just too far." Jack's words break with quick sharp gasps, holding back a cough, catching any weakness, showing so much weakness. He could not show too much he thought. Penelope watched his battle. Her eyes smiled. He could not show too much. Even with her there for him, how could he let her love him, despite how alone he felt. How could she love this side, the second half of him. She was here for him, the only person who was not tossed away each time he changed, the one person who held his hand so tight that when he tried to let go she held tighter. She said nothing, so Jack spoke again.

"I killed him…" Jack's hand shook as he reached for another cigarette. "I killed him." Penelope tossed a lighter across the table and it bounced once and hit him in the chest, he slapped his hand to his body cupping it into his damp shirt, to his palm, fingers, flicked, softly dragged, fired, then returned to the stone table. Exhale.

Penelope smiled. "Nice toss," Jack muttered.

Penelope winked, broke into a quick laughing smile then softened her lips, softened her jaw, and leaned forward placing her adorned fingers upon Jacks dry rough hand. Jack smiled her eyes intent into his. Penelope wiped a bead of sweat off of Jack's tense forehead. Her soft lips parted as she spoke close. "Yes you did kill him," she paused, kissed the bridge of his nose then leaned back to grab a cigarette. "And no one will ever know."

Coffee and a Cigarette

Oh the wait for the mountains!
So close I can taste
morning dew
born upon gray flanks of mentors.
She will be here any moment
I know
to swoop me up
in tired glee into her automobile.
This once I shall ride
faster than my feet will carry,
for though the warmth of Mother
Earth
will breathe kinder upon
the barefooted here in the flatlands,
up there,
yes up in the magical forests
of moss and turpentine
she shall breathe a crisp cool breath.

I hear an engine now
coming from afar,
be it her?
Yes

A Sleep Beneath the Willows

and when he left the field that day
he smiled as he sees

the grass that stained his sodden shirt
the dirt ground in his knees

he brushed a leaf out from his hair
and breathed in deep and long

the taste of scent that bed his soul
of flowers that linger long

Day Two

Thirsten Cooper is a man of tower.
Walking whole now I hope,
with lover's glow as she too walks in hand.
Her head upon his barracks,
her smile amongst the angels,
bare feet soiled and strong
upon the drenched summer land of moss
hanging low.
His shadow first cost me a double eye look
at the name of the one who stood low to his front.
"Pardon miss what was your last?
Samara Celeste Guillame, ah yes,
I have two envelopes for you."
Amethyst shined within her eyes as I spoke
tightening the seam to her gashes.
As Samara flit happily away
now stood the man of sadness,
his calloused hand leaned upon the very table I sat.
I moved my water a tad.
His eyes cast down into mine wondering why
must he stand here 'mongst so much pain
with no other choice but to pray and to wait.
"What is your name" I spoke almost coarse
forgetting
perhaps this man lived through the worst.
"Thirsten Cooper."
The whisper of a man who wished not to speak.
I looked up into his black lonely eyes,
oil refilled the vein they were spilled
tears clung upon one lonely orchid in snow.
I set my pen, my busy mind,

all other thoughts aside.
"Lemme check if you have mail Thirsten,"
"That's why I'm here,"
his sarcasm not for his intention was clear,
"Where is my wife?" with powerful rasp.
"If anything has come in I'll have it here..."
Thumbing my way through the cartons of letters
from family concerned and FEMA money returned
to the ones whose lives had been lost.
Though as some would see
there is a little bird in the morn
singing from the only tree
-the sky having forgotten the storm.
Dotson back
Carver continue
Cooper
Cooper Etta
Cooper Marv
Cooper Nadine
Curtis.
No Thirsten.
I double combed back and forward, no avail.
"No Thirsten Cooper I'm sorry man,
hopefully tomorrow, check back again."
Dark tower of sadness walked patiently away,
path stern to his cot,
past rows of the others,
there he lay down and closed his sad eyes.
Two paws of wait upon timbered chest.
"Brenda Billings!" her sharp cheer
slapped me back.
Up I looked into cheerful saddened quirk,
"Brenda yes!"
Down again into my droves of letters

sent for the line of tired masses
of dinner eater's with
no dishes to clean
for there is no kitchen to clean them in,
or have cooked for the babes
with deserved mothers pride
of okra, rice and spice in the bowl,
'I would have chopped 'em onions finer'
I've more than twice been told.
But Brenda, Brenda Billings,
"Yes my dear, here you are."
She winked in glee and grasped the letter
that Thirsten wasn't sent.
The line before me stood still 1,000 deep,
of angry saddened heart's unable to sleep.
The night marched on,
Lake Charles did not rest,
its liquid skin freckled by cat tails, lily pads,
souls of families displaced.
An alligator snatched a muskrat
beneath the moonlight.
Thirsten Cooper never slept.
As the sun rose pain continued to blossom.

Kiss

Some moments are unparalleled with any other seconds of anticipation, as the one when two breaths mix before lips even touch.

This undeniably perfect linger.

Both breaths dance together, quietly, heavily, slowly, not too soft to dismiss intense yearn, but quiet enough to not drown out the heart beat just inches away, separated only by soft skin, which soon too will be touched.

The breaths change from two to one as lips first graze each other, barely touching, just enough to feel her warmth, to sense any quiver that flows through her body and up to the mouth that has beautifully teased a thousand times with only a smile.

Hand raises and softly holds the bottom of her chin feeling the goddess-ness of her delicate jaw, to guide lips to her lips. Strawberry taste rushes through entire body to soul, lips strengthen and hold, one of hers above one of mine, the other of hers beneath one of mine.

We breathe deeply and grab our holds tighter, the other hand searching for the lonely skin of her back, fingering beneath the trim of her shirt to slide an arm around her waist and pull her closer. Any space between both bodies seems too much space, unwanted space, we move tighter to expel it.

Her arms wrap around my neck to lock in, lips get wetter, breaths are forfeited for the sake of lips.

As I pull her upon my lap with one arm around her waist she looks into me, hair disheveled, threatening to the hide the coca cola in her eyes. No space, keep expelling space, she bites her lower lip which glistens from the wet of mine, she refuses to let go.

Her legs wrap around my waist our bodies entwined with eyes locked on the other into the one moment which is so unparalleled with any other seconds of anticipation.

We breathe steady, heavy and slow, ready for bodies to melt into another kiss.

Remember You

I will not always be a saddened wolf
retreating to thickets.

I will not always fall apart,
on the street,
on my couch,
in your bed.
Better alone where no one knows.
Thank you for that time though.
I will not always be angry for the dead,
though I mourn
I laugh too.
Sometimes my laugh turns into you,
like today when I was shootin pool,
like tonight as I burned some pine,
I cried.
I too laughed, mourning you.
In your honor always.
Perhaps you too are laughing.
There is much to travel.
We still have the mountains, ocean and sky.
You are a cardinal now.
As Willie says kinda,
they will remain only those before us.
So I add,
and perhaps a bird.

Jacob

The calloused balls of my armored bare feet sank into the soft cool soil of the Vermont earth. My head low, intimate with the baby flames I had just created. I breathed life into the embers. "Howdy." I spoke without yet seeing the being who had just approached and stood above me.

"How did you hear me? I tried to walk as quietly as I could." His young voice bounced with excitement.

I looked up to a boy with a smooth face and eyes that told this was his first night in the woods. "I hear everything."

"Well I walked on my toes trying not to break a single twig; I wasn't trying to creep on you I just wanted to see if I could."

I smiled understandingly. The fire roared with one last long concentrated breath deep from my lungs.

He swung his clean pack onto the ground and walked over to me. I stood and held out my hand pleased that his return shake was solid with fervor. "My name is Jacob."

"Hot Wing." I replied.

"You must be a thru-hiker, which makes you the first I have met."

"I will be a thru-hiker in 500 miles."

His head tilted to the side, "ah I see. You started in Georgia then?"

"Yes."

"When?" He sat down downwind, dodging the smoke that swarmed his head, reassessed and sat closer to me in the dirt.

"April 10."

"Dang.. April feels so far away to me now. But so does yesterday…" I looked up as his voice faded and looked into his eyes. The black in them ran deep, a dark tunnel into a ravenous turmoil in his head. I could feel the weight that came not with the parting light and the blanket of night, but from those black eyes. "Do you care if I camp here as well for the night?"

"Of course not, the water is good here." I cut up spiced salami with my knife and offered Jacob some. He accepted and unpacked his freshly stuffed pack. I watched him as I ate. His fingers shook as he opened a pot that had never been used. His jaw clenched and eyes squeezed tight in a long blink. "Are you hiking the whole Long Trail?" My interest realigned his thoughts, he opened his eyes.

"Yes, I hope to. This will be my first trail, other than day trips you know?"

I nodded, "you came to the right place. It is so beautiful when you are alone surrounded by the towering pines, and the air is wet with fog."

Jacob smiled, "The Appalachian Trail and Long Trail run together for about 100 miles right?"

"Correct." I packed my pipe smoked then offered it to the rookie. He accepted, we cooked and ate, discussing every aspect of backpacking life, how to hang a bear bag, how to tell which berries and mushrooms are good to eat. What I had seen on my journeys, of wild animals, girls we wanted to love, and how to make fire. I enjoyed giving him knowledge I had learned, confident that this boy would adapt well, he fired back with questions thirsty for more, but also to avoid what lay beneath.

"Do you ever get scared alone out here at night?" He asked.

"Sometimes."

"Do you always hike alone?"

"I like to."

"Is this your first big adventure?"

"No," I smiled.

"Well it is mine."

"You are young. You have your entire life to adventure."

"This is true... Why do you hike?" This time his eyes fought back tears that had returned beneath his brow.

"Well," I started slowly, staring at the sky believing my words were at this moment monumentally important. I did not know what hurt him so badly deep inside, but I had pain that would leak out of my heart and bring me to my knees. I knew the tight long squeeze of the eyes, burying the ache back into the deepest recesses of thought not allowing it to come out any further. "I hike because it is the only place where I can start to understand everything inside of me. Standing alone on top of a mountain I can let go, and let the wind shoot right through my body and take everything away from me, until I am just one with the earth as the shimmering leaves that shake until they can hold no longer then float to the floor where we now sit. I feel free only here. I am less when I am not in the woods or surrounded by living beauty. Therefore, I do not want to be anywhere else. At home when I feel it coming on, I sink into my couch beneath blankets of misunderstanding why I cannot, or I pace around like a wild animal for hours." I stopped and looked at Jacob. He said nothing but leaned forward waiting for more. I laughed changing to a lighter mood. "Plus many other little reasons, like personal challenge, my insatiable desire to know what is over the next peak, or what new world lies at the bottom of each ravine. If I had lived before I would have been Davy Crockett, a great explorer, a pirate poet, or one simply willing to die if it meant falling off the edge of the world." I laughed and looked up to see Jacob staring into the fire. I ceased talking and lit a cigarette.

"I want to learn peace like that. I am going to hike for two reasons that I know." His black eyes danced back and forth watching the flames. "I have always wanted to hike, but I never could before. Now I can."

"Why now?" I asked.

The words did not come at first, but when they did each syllable was slow and crisp. "My mother died in a car crash last week." Jacob's lip quivered, his jaw again clenched, but did not hide his wet eyes, he looked right at me. "So now she is dead, and I cannot take care of her anymore. She was already sick. I always knew she would die, but it wouldn't be for years. After my mother's funeral I did not know what to do. I knew what I should do, I have school, and I am not the only one whose mother has died... I don't want to see my father, he never took care of her, it was just me. I had to leave everything..."

"I am so sorry Jacob."

"She was killed instantly they said. Which is best I suppose, I just wanted it to be a lie. A terrible joke would be better, if it was just a terrible joke, or dream. Because I don't know what I am going to do, I am sitting here on the dirt alone with you, which is better than being anywhere else because when I sat on that damn wooden bench looking at my mother's casket, and each person hugged me I felt none of it. I couldn't speak of any of it. I miss her so much. I just miss her so much. The last thing she told me was 'Jacob I love you,' and she kissed my forehead and I pulled away quick like, laughing, because she would always try to get me, then out the door I ran. She was killed an hour later." Jacob buried his head into his hands and cried. I sat there as tears fell down my face not knowing how to help, or if I should say anything at all. He said no more, just stood up to set his tent then returned sitting next to me again.

We stared silently at the fire and listened to the night. My heart hurt for this young boy, I could not fix him, but I knew he was in the right place. Sometimes the finest cure for pain is to be alone with the woods. I fed the embers a last log and finally broke the long silence. "Tomorrow will be good, mountain tops and lush springs all day."

"Yes, it will be good." Jacob smiled, dirt caked on his dried salty cheeks, "I'm going to turn in for the night, how far you planning on hiking tomorrow?"

"Probably about 23 miles," I answered.

"Do you get up early?"

"Depends, I wake when I'm rested I sleep when I am tired."

Jacob chuckled, "no rules out here huh?"

"You got it pal."

"Alright Hot Wing, goodnight, thank you." I looked at Jacob, he spoke once more. "And you know how you said if you lived before you would have been a great explorer?"

"Yeah?"

"Well, that is a stupid thing to say because you already are."

I laughed gentle as his kind words touched my soul.

"Goodnight Jacob."

He grabbed his pack and meandered through the dark towards his tent; I listened to his long sighs and prayed his mind could find a way to rest tonight. I leaned back and laid flat on the earth my feet warm from the tired fire. I thought of my mother until I slipped into sleep.

Midnight Jaunts

Walked home again tonight
as I do,
beneath fresh waning moon.
On nights as these after long work on feet
I stop into my last option store
n buy my first option brew.
To live upon this land,
to eat, drink, smoke of its milk and honey,
a choice IPA I choose.
Then uphill I face with constant step forward
into the always darker land I sip and sing,
I smoke n joke out loud with the lions,
shadows and arms that reach.
"Oh this man's a walkin,
a walkin that never ends.
For once you walk the country
seems I forever walk it again!"
Aye what a blessing,
a blessing indeed.
Here in my hall,
silver kingdom of alligator pillars
above turpentine beds,
another swig n toke
raised scalp to the waning fresh
I howl.
"Here in the west I abide,
here in the west I live,
here in the west I laugh and cry,
here in the west I rise my head."

Hideaway

gurgling drawl

better far away

life lines of hobos

seeking the asphalt way

but in this pocket hush of willows

where wind drifts 'tween

humble bow

cattail strong

enough to give muscles upon

bones,

strength to prolong

another day

another day

Kid from the Shire

First strode into Bend on foot,
then by truck,
ne'er by train.
kid of the shire,
met another the same.
Aspens of my earth all grown apart,
creature from same lands, other lands
may always share my hearth.
The strange empty gut of time that has truly past;
the ache of a remembrance
which bares no resemblance.

Dead is not dead

as does spring and the sap and rivers rise,
despite my other lives,
get back to the trail.
Sweat the alcohol gone.
There are berries ahead never tasted,
tree trunks ne'er seen,
forever been buried by
lonesome no change past.
A new horse,
a new gun,
a new bag of smoke,
into the silver tipped forlorn of never met.
With the Shire and whomever may
light my north.

The Commons

Met a man a year ago today
right here with his beer
                         and dog
who has a few more greys
a few more good memories
if dogs choose to remember fondly

Yes, after work he first brought
a bowl of water to the happy shaggy
brown black and grey

then only after responsibilities attended
does he get his own deserved frosty beverage

Like before he is now,
a kind quip about the season change
a sarcastic slight at how terrible a day,
with a smile.

Then

my conscious now is a
compilation   of
        single magic breaths
each an avalanche
        of love
                and frustration
upon a mountain shrouded
by old man beard
        'neath ominous fangs
veiling struggled
        submission
        to serenity

oh presence of peace
warm butter dreaming into bread
sharp cheddar atop

September

purple musk
        dinosaur bellows
        from each direction
silver chill
        conifer cackles
        pressing the green
ebony wet
        will still exist
        come lunch number two
        as will toes blue
        river forge of
                grey gurgles
                white dancing
                diamonds
                if the sun breaks
                through
meadows promise such
        providing eastern views
        of rays far away

back into the fog
back into his sanctuary

he bellows ahead
        quiet feet continue
he bellows closer now
        purple musk

Son of a Father

There was no rain.
No clouds to commiserate this pain;
just the sun upon foreheads
above the black suits
and formal shoes
covered in dust
until yesterday.

My father spoke of his father.
I beheld my father
as I held his father.

With chin up and chest out,
with love that poured upon
this weighted wood.
I held the mentor,
the giver of life.

I then knew.
I too,
want a son.

Portsmouth Fire

Oh to be where the lightning strikes so,
in the air that is fire of living young souls.
The streets that are drenched
with spilled summer sand,
once stuck to her legs from 5 drinks ago.
Blond hearted angels kiss the tanned chest
as we are stained by the wet
of a summer undressed.
So dance I will for this is our time,
damn future rot shan't salute such decline;
This is our time and these souls are my please,
of Portsmouth New Hampshire
and its home dancing disease.

Dab City

Perhaps I'd be working, each name and drink and foreseeable problem n fortune knowing. To serve the community rightly I must be honestly loose and succumbing to suggestion, gifts, bowls, joints, blunts, joints, dabs, porch dabs all day porch dabs, I do better on my wit that way. Suppose Mitul walks into the bar, I recognize and mentally prepare. Dab City. "Hot Wing take a dab." He'd say after I'd fill up his second pint of half imperial stout and half double IPA. "You just gave me a dab, dab city brotha I walked in the gates just minutes ago." "Another two quick dabs Hot Wing." His big bear smile and the way pint glass clung to his sticky fingers. "Aye give me a bit; let's wait 'til the crew hits the porch." The crew was thirsty. Red IPA to the back, already pouring 3 single Cali's for town family up front, damn she's cute this one's on me, a double jack A, sour sister for her, and him, taste for me, they ain't bad. Dab City what's bad? Andy wants a stone, I know he wants a stone and more he wants his music, hell yeah man lets rock n roll!! Music too loud, perhaps for some, I see three stouts low in the back so I prepare, when they look at my eye I'm already there. Blacksmith. Fire chief. My brother at home, these beers are for you to hopefully keep you warm. South Carolina n Chris I got you, "what the heck Frank! Where'd you go to!?" With an Arnie and two Geno's I see the eye from the back, two long haired dirt bikers aiming for the porch, Loopy always leading the force. All beers have been

served, the crew and I cheer, with drink we do
relinquish days long, then to Dab City we return.

Caribou Hill

here arrows feathered sinful chests
heathen blood spilled out of necks
as blades mated jugulars
scalps exposed brains

here white has raped red
human has raped human
making the latter's anger justified
yet pure retaliation
deemed savage
so eliminate for gold
for holes deep into God's belly
in His name

here darkness loomed amidst the promises
amidst land that is not his nor hers
despite disbelief

for what we claim is ours, yes?
what we choose is right must be right
to govern other men and woman as we feel fit
though that government is not.

I am the land and the sky,
I am the green.

The one true governor will remain
the rest shall fade away.

Bang Bang

We celebrate with bangs.
As we should.
It is just
to be excited
in something we believe
to be right.
Though we then turn and terrorize
the first dark shadow.
The shadow put down is then
the bang.
I do believe we shall never see him again.
Let freedom ring!
Is the words I heard most sing
as they ride in a circle to let the other clang.
Bang bang.
Two more you shall never see.
It does not matter.
They are the shadow
they are the murk
the last tie to our morality,
so let us continue on with indifference.
A smashing of insults upon our own selves
I could assault.
But rather I would lay here and take
them all myself.
For in my ditch as I lay dying
I am never offended.
A smile upon my face,
no war upon each other.

For we all are just trying to cherish

not being in the ditch and dying.
So go celebrate you fools
who feel the need to exhibit this very ideal of life.
Try not to kill each other this time.
Or,
bang bang.

Cattail Wallows

I tread
in the fragile tundra
of right and wrong,
between death and life.
The former merely
a misunderstanding
of the latter.

This is no transition song
simply
an observation
of what we call being.

I am strongly conflicted
by the morality
of our own selves,
it seems to be a reverse affect
upon the very definition of life.

No wonder we die.

Red Ribbon Haze

such a dismembered
oddly understood
parallel craze

in my lacey star dacey space

it continued like this
with the midnight walker
North Star stalker
earth rejuvenated
by fairy dancing feet
celebrating the moon
avec autumns raucous beat

red is the color I see
midst these golden halls
of yellow and green
ribbon red wrapping it all
eyeball opals
discover new portals
into a visible conjugation
of tortured soul mutilated

but ah no more midnight man
no more-
you are the North Star stalker forgiven
the autumn hall walker,
in this red ribbon haze
you will begin again

An Art Thought, a Life Goal

That is the thing with art,
when inspiration strikes
you are doomed
to the glory of your craft.
To put off brilliance
is to let pasta cook to mush,
to let the vindication of four words
perhaps be there tomorrow
is the girl you did not consort.

Mismatched earrings no socks

a malachite now in her pocket.

Do not over cook the pasta,
tell her of the wild she stirs.
We who are mad
have an understanding with less,
no more than the breeze
to live a time far away,
imagination of youth,
oh the pilgrimage it has been!
I must live.
I shall sit here on rocks and consider
their patient silence
then walk towards the horizon forever.

Puddle Straw

there he stands
towering above
a Pillar Thor
or puddle straw
a giant sad
all alone
born out of hope
and dinosaur bone
reaching beneath
dormant energy
defying the wrath
winter will bring
ignoring haunted souls
of brothers beneath
the petrified death
of lava breath

No Buttons

This flannel doesn't have any buttons
but that's okay.
I like the breeze on my chest anyway,
and the gawks n the smiles,
the midday head shakes,
he should be creating wealth for others
some seem to say.
I like them too, the lookers and the looks.
No buttons,
for my dog had decided
it was time my 2nd favorite shirt
became a drape.
No more hug for you
from such fabric you dig,
only hug in this world is this bitch,
so she said.
So,
happily I let my mammal chest breathe
past the collared n ties of corporate greed,
past a favorite lil Mexican joint
where I usually show up,
after smoking a joint,
but not today for I'm down to the river
for a wholesome good time
of poems and water.

My chest flies with
no buttons to hide
life living zeal n
modern walking prose.

Past all the shops filled with
back packs and shoes,
past the pizza slices with
beaucoup toppings to choose,
past the pipes debonair
where stoners and me
examine the glass
considering our piece.

Past seven breweries,
gonna grab a beer at the 8th,
but first I must slither through
empty tourist space.
Past the chocolatier
and t shirts of town,
past
Hold on.
Wait.
Ima get a chocolate.

The Routine of Two Feet

The day started much like any other. My eyes opened slowly at 5:45 am to a dim-lit Yosemite sky. The same fluid sound I fell asleep to still caresses my ears of cold fresh water meandering its way through the lush narrow valley. I lift my head and consider unzipping the flap on my tent. The mosquitos would not be awake yet, but I declined as the cold air convinced my limbs to stay tucked in my warm sleeping bag. I could see about anyway. My rain fly lay at my feet as usual, I cocooned by the see-through mesh of my Marmot tent which helped to avoid the bugs. Had I slept above this valley upon the granite crests free of gnats I would have let my tired body sleepily melt into the ground beneath an intimate meeting with the stars.

I stretch my toes and legs out as far and straight as ligaments would allow. Pleased with my body, happy to not wake up sore anymore, for each day I felt stronger than the last. Everything in me felt healthy, my deep long breaths, both knees, each joint, my tight dependable core, my appetite. Still managing to keep most of my skin inside my sleeping bag I rolled a morning cigarette, lit it and indulged my mind upon that strong appetite of mine. I loved mornings such as these. No one had moved in on my camp spot while I was sleeping during the night so I was still completely alone. I would lay here, read a bit, then after my cigarette blow life into the lukewarm embers of my little fire ring and cook up a feast for breakfast. Two-thousand calories would be my goal for a kick start meal as 30 miles would be my goal for the mountain trekking day.

Two packets of chocolate powdered protein with whole milk powder and a healthy squeeze of olive oil shaken up with cold flowing mountain water to begin. Next a can of chili, two granola bars that I carefully selected from my collection of seven, a handful of gummy worms, the rest of my Goldfish bag I stashed into my pocket for later. Still hungry I looked at all of my options that I had lain about. With no desire to eat a packet of instant mashed potatoes, I chose to slap some peanut butter and honey on a couple flour tortillas instead. Two-thousand calories down I felt the energy surging back into my body. I left an apple out of my pack to pair with the Goldfish for a snack on the go.

As I sat by my morning fire and ate, the sun had adequate time to rise above the granite wall to my east. Its warm rays turned each droplet of dew into silver dancing steam rising out of my sleeping bag and scattered clothes. I began to pack in the same manner per usual, first putting each item into its appropriate zip lock or stuff sack, sleeping bag always stuffed down into the deepest recesses of my pack, next my tent, then each item in its due order. By the end of the process everything was where it should be. My pack was completely balanced and organized. As the last flickering coals surrendered I dropped onto the dirt and did my first set of pushups for the day, time to hike.

The first three miles would be a three thousand foot climb up to a mountain pass. Here I would descend into another northern valley of marvel, surely. Everything smelled fresh and clean, a brand new day in Yosemite had awoken. Periodically the sun's rays glistened upon thin wisps of spider webs that were draped across the trail. Thankful for the warning I simply twirled my walking stick in front of me, breaking each one away before they stuck to my beard, neck or forearms. In the shadows I was not as fortunate, but I smiled knowing I was the first to walk the trail this morning. I picked my feet up onto solid rocks lodged in the dusty ground climbing higher with each step. Looking back down the trail behind I acknowledged, "this land needs rain." A ground squirrel chirped approval and dashed across the trail as the loose dirt we had kicked up failed to settle quickly.

As each mile passed my muscles warmed and extra layers donned from the cool morning were stripped. I was atop the pass within an hour. High alpine passes always mean new scenery, new canyons and magical land to explore on the other side. Down I skipped into my new valley of wilderness until I reached a fast moving river, dropped my pack, tore off my boots, socks and clothes and jumped into the cold Sierra water. As I was scrubbing my dirty body clean another's eyes set upon my back. I turned to look but saw nothing, his being flickering upon the intangible energy field. After moment's close watch I saw him move, a mighty Black Tailed Deer, a grandfather of fortune, a king of the forest, a wise regal buck, giant rack of sharp sabers crowned the royal head. His chin lifted high and his eyes bore confidently into mine. My bath must have interrupted his morning drink but I never frightened him for, why would I? We both were citizens to the wilderness and he knew that. My smell and step was not city or danger; it was of another creature at home. We conversed for a moment; I dressed, ate my apple and moved along.

Afternoon brought me deep into ancient mountain ravines then steeply back up over forested passes. As I descended again I found myself in a thickly wooded virginal forest. Firs and cedars tower above allowing my passage no longer. Thick majestic trunks of dense wood rose a hundred feet into the sky. Boughs sweeping laterally through clean filtered air were sleeved with thick luscious green, yellow, silver, brown, white and black mosses. The forest floor was littered with these fallen giants, upon thick beds of green they lay. The giants of old fed the soil for roots of now and giants of tomorrow, making the trail nearly impassable. I climbed up and over, crawled under and around until reaching a small intersection. 'Benson Lake home of the Benson Riviera' the old wooden post told, it was just .4 miles to my west. With eager childlike glee I turned from my home of the Pacific Crest Trail, to a demon disguised. My doom lay just ahead.

Father

This reminds me of you,
frosted blades of tall wild grass
a barely breathing glow upon it all,
hot black coffee on my knee.

Like those New England mornings we spent,
for you brought me there.
The owl we searched for now satisfied
from a feast we all shared.

To this day I'd rather use an axe to split wood,
a shovel to move snow
from one place to another
than any machine less fit.
So strong this mind and body
with patience practiced.

Perhaps if not for those long walks
from stony ridge
to wet beaver logged hollow
I would be less hungry now
for the magical marvel of truth in the wind.

Perhaps if not for your limitless love
as an eagle rising above night laden sea
'til you reach tomorrows sun,
my zealous love for life
would never be.

No Light Upon My Porch

Crickets singing,
sun has set for the day.
To the east
a thunderstorm sprawls and speaks
whispering the secrets
I wished they would say.
The wolf pups are phased
by none of it
'cept the persistent neighbor dog
they run off every 5 minutes.
Miles Davis,
smoke
and wine.
This is one of those
good sides of Georgia.

Night with the Devil

The devil looked him in the eyes with a patient strength, a tone as deep as tender filled with both remorse and challenge.

'So you are sure this is what you want?'

The man nodded and held the devil's eyes in his own, redder than the sweetest rose and blacker than the deepest sea.

"You will not join me yet then." The devil leaned back casually assaulting the man's fervency.

" I will not join you ever." The man hissed through the fire which flickered between them. This was his fire, his wood, within mountains upon a mountain, in a ravine on the westernmost flank, here alone with the devil. The man raised the warm whiskey to his sun beaten lips and took another long drink. He turned the meat that lay on grate above the flames. It spat and sizzled as virgin flesh now bore their faces to hell. Another drink. The devil treaded in silence across the fire, slunk back upon a log. A gentle smile seemed to rest across his unfathomable face, his eyes never left the man. He was in no hurry to leave, as often is the case but here! In this forest of peace beneath these giant trees of time!

'Trees of time?' The devil scoffed. 'There is no time; your soul is my time!' The devils poisonous laugh echoed off the steep granite cliffs of the mountains. Rocks dislodged from their temporary rest to tumble further down the gorge. The lions retreated, the bears stood still and watched as a fierce righteous anger brewed within the man's soul.

Daughter of Eternal Clocks

the leaves have begun to fall again
from the velvet green of beaded sweat
when clothes seemed an unreasonable option
to the crisp yellow of blue wool upon the neck

wrap me in your blanket baby
there's room beneath for two
let the winter winds seep deep
down into summer's tomb

look at the leaves baby
three have fallen upon your lap
may they never touch the ground
it is you they've touched at last

oh look at this orange now
mystified by your locks
it seems you are the autumn soul
the Daughter of Eternal Clocks

she held me close within the blue
the wool both on our necks
but just as summer has sighed reprieve
so the wind takes her with my breath

brown flutter of leaves dissemble
upon my weathered nose
char of yesterday
vanishing into unknown

standing as a hobbled man

beard not quite as long
I follow the howl of hollows entreating
into the darkness

where trees do the haunting

Symphony of Youth

Eye holds steady upon the polestar,
as if my beneath willow sleep
shall suddenly be jolted.
For I descended the mountain to a deep dark hole
and mourned the symphony of youth.
Even hell may not be this
I lied
beneath shredded skin.

But that was yesterday,
for today though I go crazy
it is simply to stay sane.
I have climbed
and with Herculean tasks to render,
to fix what death will not,
to sow and feed good which naught doesn't,
I live.

Cling to Life

I do not know what my future holds,
though I bear tenacious zest for life
and I hold the rudder -
I am not the wind.
She is much stronger
He the decider.
On knoll I imagine
paradise beyond the pass,
a new valley of magic
to where I walk and run
'til I am here at last.
Beneath Bristle Cone Pine
I have a vision
of a world more holy and kind
full of loving intention.
High in alpine lands
I laugh tingled by joy
alive upon her breast
away from the machine that churns
destroying ideals of justice
away from the angst of
misguided unrest.
I long to inspire,
I react to the sad and the passionate
to the wild bursting hearts
that can't be explained.
Ah a future I am never in beyond now!
Are my nightmares the truth of
another today,
are my fantasies realities just not quite yet?
For I sure as hell won't wait to see

what an ill induced fate may bring.
I am in full climbing speed
from a grave I'll never dig
responding to the beat
of my rowdy heart songs.
Where I am is where I am
despite the life crimes
despite Atlas weight
despite disappointment to another.
Were they even blunders if what was is is
and that is is now!
Perhaps mistakes are the most honest form of us.
I shall be honest in return,
I grieve silently for every single heart I have hurt.
Ground beneath a giant millstone
my pain never fades
only compounds and cocoons
until I climb a mountain alone
and cry upon the nipples of mother earth.
Only then do my tears turn into butterflies
and return as sunsets and songs
and memories of life lived.
Stronger I am today than yesterday
both my heart and my cough.
Stronger I shall be tomorrow
and though I am no crystal ball king
though I am not the wind
I am the legacy of my mother and father.
I am brother to Michael and Carmen.
I am the creation of all sooted beneath
the millstone of pain.
Dust crawl to the trees
kaleidoscope drinkers scatter us again
we the makings of a trillion women and men,

I the beating heart of all others that have beat
I not blue or yellow
I've decided I am green.
That makes us family
all you who share this beat,
we each are the other
with each own soul unique.
I the legacy of all we know
you the legacy too,
so, though we may not know tomorrow
let us live today.
Let us strip the rust of hate
out of our hearts and now,
let us be rudders of kindness and love.

Poem Box

I had not been here long
when I first stumbled upon
a poem box.
Poem of the month it read,
though no poem within.
Placed above a bench
attached to adobe,
on the corner of a corner.
Delaware.
Sad to see no poem inside
I strode along in decision
to walk my dog
this way again.
Perhaps next time…
The skeleton souls awakened.
Sap began to rise.
As my dog and I meandered
there continued to be
no poems inside.
I took a step back
which I've always found valuable,
analyzed,
considered,
decided to dive into my idea.
This building so quaint,
this corner on a corner.
This shall be my poem box,
least 'til other dance hither
as I always hope,
I shall dance alone
but it would be a delight

if you too would dance with me,
and so it was.
My first poem about thankfulness,
community.
Second a lesson learned
from climbing a tree.
My pursuit purposeful
through all of these.
Now as I ramble home,
a man with a dog
or without, then
a man missing his dog;
I tumble by my poem box
with another poem to drop.
Always wishing next time
there shall be
more than me.

Little Woodland Savage

boy on his birthday
buster brown
of New England ground
peak of each autumn
on a hike through the leaves

to find the cave he dwells in.

apple cinnamon goods baked
cube of maple syrup candy
semen of the tree
wrapped in flannel lined hat
case the wind bites his ear

tunes of yesterday
playing in the brain
cello now reminds me
of all the piano hours he played
on crisp windy nights

after a hunt for the cave.

telling Mother of his finds
chin in the steam
bellow between bites
devouring hot pot roast
little woodland savage
eating potato tender
seeking new frontiers
carrot fingers
hands half washed

onion nearly clear
before the last hill crest
he could smell her love
cooked slow on low,
perhaps a bay leaf in the juice

"Remember son there are wild animals in these
woods. I know you are keen but the bear or wildcat
may find you as you find the roast!"

family feline black and white
sleuth upon piano
jumps to my side
purring saunter
rub for hello

Just years in turn he would himself be brought to
bodied doom by the latter of her fears.

"Ah Mother but hear!"
another bellow between bites
of new birds recorded
that quickly creeping autumn night,
"they see me not as foe
but as tender walking soul
let the bear within the cave
kindly show himself
let the cougar or the fisher-cat
both watch me sit
whispering beaver's busy hymns
bending with reed in the wind
upon side of the marsh tan
the Great Blue Heron he knows
I mean no harm,

my whistle and my sing
get melodic responses from
each winged being!"

she stopped me short
Mother's loving counsel

"It is not just the bear in the cave
you must respect my son,
fingers with flour to her heart,
it is too the bear within."

Poison Ivy on a Good Day

A hug that clings around my neck
of love that brews despite its wreck,
kisses linger of time long before
with scent of chance and her adore.
O'er mountains far her visage stayed true,
through time and trees
sterling love well grew,
to melt my strength upon her sight
she is my strength for life's one plight,
that goddess face to kiss and hold
her skin and lust my lips one gold,
a love so far, buried beneath haunted moors,

yet forever she will be, my amour.

The Singing Tree

Hawthorn golden yellow
red blue and leftover green
paint his leaves still clinging,
melatonin woody creature
more stubborn than other trees
for they all have
bowed to November
but not the Hawthorn man
who still shimmers
with Indian Summer days,
no not this stubborn sage
who understands the warming of the land.

Short solid trunk
thick and slightly gnarled
splits into four new arms
two thicker make a shallow V,
the other ligaments hang
shorter, baring
nimble fingers
rounding out his skeleton dress,
upon each four siblings extend
a mire of shoots
each at their ends
stubborn painted oakiness glitter.

A handsome tree he is
kind handsome host
the singing tree,
for within this giant nest past noon
before the sun has bid adieu

I cannot even count one-hundred
before
the birds they flutter and double
some in song
some in chatter
goldfinch the former
sparrows the latter,
God's golden Hawthorn which
too filters veiny blue
is in this sunlight draped
by majestic singing troupe.

Stand and Listen

You find me in a quiet place,
with gentle wind,
with conversations within.
You find me blowing life into the sparks,
nurturing a boldness through tacit,
nurturing belief of greatness into such.
Seeming soft laden rest,
there is not.
Peace emanates though zeal is the spark.
What bloom it shall become
I do not yet know,
for it is the nurturing still all I know,
though it shall be
God's art to behold.

www.ingramcontent.com/pod-product-compliance
Lightning Source LLC
Chambersburg PA
CBHW070620050426
42450CB00011B/3088